Plant Parts

Stems

Revised Edition

by Vijaya Khisty Bodach

Consulting Editor: Gail Saunders-Smith, PhD

Consultant: Judson R. Scott, Former President
American Society of Consulting Arborists

CAPSTONE PRESS
a capstone imprint

Pebble Plus is published by Capstone Press,
1710 Roe Crest Drive, North Mankato, Minnesota 56003.
www.capstonepub.com

Copyright © 2007, 2016 by Capstone Press, a Capstone imprint. All rights reserved.

No part of this publication may be reproduced in whole or in part, or stored in a retrieval system, or transmitted in any form or by any means, electronic, mechanical, photocopying, recording, or otherwise, without written permission of the publisher. For information regarding permission, write to Capstone Press, 1710 Roe Crest Drive, North Mankato, Minnesota 56003.

Library of Congress Cataloging-in-Publication Data is available on the Library of Congress website.

ISBN: 978-1-5157-4247-0 (revised paperback)
ISBN: 978-1-5157-4356-9 (ebook pdf)

Editorial Credits
Sarah L. Schuette, editor; Jennifer Bergstrom, designer; Kelly Garvin, photo researcher/photo editor

Photo Credits
Capstone Studio: Karon Dubke, Cover, 5; Getty Images: Kim Heacox, 13; Shutterstock: 1000 Words, right 22, Africa Studio, 19, Alexey Lisovoy, 11, kaczor58, left 22, Lancelot et Naelle, background 15, Rudolf Georg, 21, sirano 100, 1, Tarashevskiy, 7, Yevgen Chornobay, (bulb) 15, yuris, 17, zastavkin, 9

Note to Parents and Teachers

The Plant Parts set supports national science standards related to identifying plant parts and the diversity and interdependence of life. This book describes and illustrates stems. The images support early readers in understanding the text. The repetition of words and phrases helps early readers learn new words. This book also introduces early readers to subject-specific vocabulary words, which are defined in the Glossary section. Early readers may need assistance to read some words and to use the Table of Contents, Glossary, Read More, Internet Sites, and Index sections of the book.

Table of Contents

Plants Need Stems............ 4
All Kinds of Stems........... 10
Stems We Eat 16
Wonderful Stems 20

Parts of an Oak Tree 22
Glossary 23
Read More 23
Index 24
Internet Sites.............. 24

Plants Need Stems

Stems join the leaves and roots of a plant. Most stems grow above the soil.

5

Leaves grow from stems.
Stems hold leaves up
to the sun.
Leaves make food
out of sunlight.

Stems act like straws.

They carry food

from the leaves and roots

to the whole plant.

All Kinds of Stems

Tall, woody tree trunks are stems covered with bark. The bark protects the stem.

Strawberry plants have long, thin stems. The stems creep along on top of the soil.

Tulip bulbs
are underground stems.
In spring, leaves grow up
and tulips bloom.

bulb

Stems We Eat

Some stems are good to eat.

Celery stems are

a crunchy snack.

Asparagus stems grow quickly.

These stems are called spears.

Wonderful Stems

Woody or soft, thick or thin, stems help plants stay alive.

Parts of an Oak Tree

seed

roots

leaves

stem

Glossary

bulb—an underground stem; tulips grow from bulbs.

leaves—the flat, green parts of a plant that grow out from a stem

root—the part of a plant that grows mostly underground; food gathered by roots moves through stems to the rest of the plant.

soil—the dirt where plants grow; most plants get their food and water from the soil.

Read More

Farndon, John. *Stems.* World of Plants. San Diego: Blackbirch Press, 2005.

Hunter, Rebecca. *The Facts About Flowering Plants.* North Mankato, Minn.: Smart Apple Media, 2005.

Morgan, Sally. *Green Plants.* Life Science In Depth. Chicago: Heinemann Library, 2006.

Index

asparagus, 18

bark, 10

bulbs, 14

celery, 16

food, 6, 8

leaves, 4, 6, 8, 14

roots, 4, 8

soil, 4, 12

strawberry, 12

sunlight, 6

trunks, 10

tulips, 14

Word Count: 122
Grade: 1
Early-Intervention Level: 15

Internet Sites

FactHound offers a safe, fun way to find Internet sites related to this book. All of the sites on FactHound have been researched by our staff.

Here's how:

1. Visit www.facthound.com

2. Choose your grade level.

3. Type in this book ID 0736863478 for age-appropriate sites. You may also browse subjects by clicking on letters, or by clicking on pictures and words.

4. Click on the Fetch It button.

Facthound will fetch the best sites for you!